15 Minute Dash Die

Quick Meals for Busy People

DISCLAIMER

No part of this eBook can be transmitted or reproduced in any form including print, electronic, photocopying, scanning, mechanical or recording without prior written permission from the author.

While the author has taken utmost efforts to ensure the accuracy of the written content, all readers are advised to follow information mentioned herein at their own risk. The author cannot be held responsible for any personal or commercial damage caused by misinterpretation of information.

All information, ideas, and guidelines presented here are for educational purposes only and readers are encouraged to seek professional advice when needed

SUMMARY

Dietary approaches to stop hypertension (DASH) diet are an approach towards a balanced diet, which will help to maintain a healthier lifestyle and live longer. The DASH diets have been researched and approved to provide the claimed benefits by the National, Heart, Lung, and Blood Institute. This kind of diet includes foods, which are low in salt (sodium) and rich in nutrients, which prevent hypertension and helps lower blood pressure. Since the DASH diet includes healthy foods, it also helps to prevent other health concerns such as osteoporosis, diabetes, cancer, and heart diseases.

In this e-book, you will find DASH diet recipes, which are well researched to provide the above mentioned health benefits. These recipes as well as being beneficial for health are also delicious, and can be made in a jiffy; to be exact, just under 15 minutes.

What's more? Find Dash diet recipe for all phases, made in just 15 minutes, this eBook will give you:

1. Complete recipes with serving limit, cooking time and nutrition value
2. Dash diet recipes for all phases
3. Complete step by step directions to easily make the recipes

So read ahead, to start living a healthier life!

Contents

DISCLAIMER..2

SUMMARY 3

Buckwheat Pancakes 7

Asparagus and Caramelized Onion Frittata.............................9

Applesauce French toast 11

Fruit and Grain Breakfast Salad 13

Spinach, Mushroom and Feta Cheese Scramble 15

No bake breakfast granola bars..17

Breakfast Green Smoothie 19

Almond Date Shake..21

Berry Museli..23

Quinoa..25

Broccoli and Cheese Omelet..27

Morning Mohito...29

Cinnamon French toast 31

Apple-Swiss Panini...33

Orange Rice Salad 35

Sunshine Wraps 37

Salmon Salad Pita 39

Mayo-Less Tuna Salad...41

Pear, Turkey and Cheese Sandwich 43

Orange Rice Salad 45

Veggie Quesadillas with Cilantro Yogurt Dip	47
Yellow Lentils	49
Grilled Cod with Salad	51
White Chicken Chili	53
Chinese Noodles with Vegetables	55
Acorn Squash with Apples	57
Easy Cheesy Enchiladas	59
Festive Cranberry Chicken	61
Garden Quesadillas	63
Cilantro Lime Tilapia Tacos	65
One Pan Spaghetti	67
Cheeseburgers	69
Cowboy Salad	71
Pasta and Broccoli	73
Citrus Chicken	75
Pear Chicken Curry	77
Vegetable and Turkey Stir-Fry	79
Chicken Cabbage Stir Fry	81
Bean Dip Athenos	83
Pumpkin Pie Spiced Yogurt	85
Lemon Smoothie	87
Muffins	88
Zucchini Pizza Bites	90

Melon Cooler 92

Skillet Granola 94

Chicken Burritos 96

Tuna Pita Pockets.. 98

Garlic Potatoes 100

Apple and Pistachio Salad... 102

Pumpkin Chai Smoothie 104

Buckwheat Pancakes

SERVING SIZE

Six persons

COOKING TIME

10-15 minutes

INGREDIENTS

Egg whites: 2

Canola oil: 1 tbsp

Fat-free milk: ½ cup

All-purpose flour: ½ cup

Buckwheat flour: ½ cup

Baking powder: 1 tbsp

Sugar: 1 tbsp

Water: ½ cup

Strawberries: 3 cups

PREPARATION

1. Whisk egg whites, canola oil, and milk in a small bowl
2. Combine flour, baking powder, and sugar in another bowl. Stir in the egg white mixture and water until moistened
3. Cook ½ cup of pancake batter over non-stick frying pan until edges turn light brown for about 2 minutes on each side.
4. Cook the remaining batter and serve with sliced strawberries

NUTRITIONAL VALUE PER SERVING

Calories: 143

Fat: 3g

Protein: 5g

Carbohydrates: 24g

Asparagus and Caramelized Onion Frittata

SERVING SIZE

Four persons

COOKING TIME

15 minutes

INGREDIENTS

Olive oil: 1 tsp

Thinly sliced onion: 1 medium

Vinegar: 2 tsp

Sliced asparagus: 2 cups

Sliced green onions: 3

Thinly sliced basil: ¼ cup

Eggs: ½ dozen

Grated cheese (parmesan): ¼ cup plus 1 tbsp

Kosher salt: ½ tsp

Water: 2 tbsp

Black pepper: to taste

PREPARATION

1. Cook onions in olive oil until slightly brown. Add vinegar, asparagus, and 2 tbsp water and cover for 4 minutes to steam asparagus
2. In a medium bowl, whisk eggs, ¼ cup grated parmesan, ¼ tsp kosher salt and ground pepper.
3. Stir in green onion, basil, and remaining ¼ tsp kosher salt to cooked asparagus and onion. Add egg mixture and mix with spatula for 2 minutes
4. Serve with 1 tbsp of parmesan cheese slicing the frittata into 4 wedges

NUTRITIONAL VALUE PER SERVING

Calories: 190

Fat: 11g

Protein: 14g

Carbohydrates: 8g

Applesauce French toast

SERVING SIZE

Six persons

COOKING TIME

10-15 minutes

INGREDIENTS

Eggs: two

Milk: ½ cup

Ground cinnamon: 1 tsp

White sugar: 2 tbsp

Unsweetened applesauce: ¼ cup

Whole wheat bread: six slices

PREPARATION

1. Combine eggs, milk, cinnamon, sugar and applesauce in a large mixing bowl and mix well
2. Soak one slice at a time until it absorbs the mixture slightly.
3. Cook over medium heat until golden brown on each side and serve hot

NUTRITIONAL VALUE PER SERVING

Calories: 150

Fat: 3g

Protein: 8g

Carbohydrates: 27g

Fruit and Grain Breakfast Salad

SERVING SIZE

Six persons

COOKING TIME

15 minutes

INGREDIENTS

Water: 3 cups

Salt: ¼ tsp

Brown rice: ¾ cup

Bulgur: ¾ cup

Granny smith apple: 1

Red apple: 1

Orange: 1

Prepared raisins: 1 cup

Low fat vanilla yogurt: 8 oz

PREPARATION

1. Boil water and salt over high heat.
2. Reduce heat and cook rice and bulgur for ten minutes.
3. Set and aside and cover for 2 minutes.
4. Cut and prepare the fruits into sections before serving
5. Mix chilled grains prepared from before and cut fruit in a bowl, stir in yogurt and serve.

NUTRITIONAL VALUE PER SERVING

Calories: 187

Fat: 1g

Protein: 4g

Carbohydrates: 40g

Spinach, Mushroom and Feta Cheese Scramble

SERVING SIZE

One person

COOKING TIME

10 minutes

INGREDIENTS

Cooking spray

Sliced mushrooms: ½ cup

Chopped spinach: 1 cup

Eggs: 1 whole and 2 egg whites

Feta cheese: 2 tbsp

Pepper: to taste

PREPARATION

1. Heat pan over medium high heat, and spray with cooking spray. Add mushrooms and spinach. Sauté for 2-3 minutes.
2. In a bowl, whisk egg and egg whites with feta cheese and pepper, pour the mixture in pan and cook for 3-4 minutes, stirring with spatula.
3. Serve hot.

NUTRITIONAL VALUE PER SERVING

Calories: 150

Fat: 7g

Protein: 17g

Carbohydrates: 6g

No bake breakfast granola bars

SERVING SIZE

Eighteen persons

COOKING TIME

15 minutes

INGREDIENTS

Toasted rice cereal: 2 ½ cups

Oatmeal: 2 cups

Raisins: ½ cup

Brown sugar: ½ cup

Light corn syrup: ½ cup

Peanut butter: ½ cup

Vanilla: 1 tsp

PREPARATION

1. Stir rice cereal, oatmeal, and raisins in a bowl.
2. Stir brown sugar and corn syrup on medium high heat constantly. Remove from heat when it comes to boil.
3. Blend the peanut butter and vanilla into the sugar mixture in saucepan until smooth.
4. Mix the peanut butter mixture with cereal and raisins well.
5. Press mixture into baking pan and cut into 18 bars after it cools.

NUTRITIONAL VALUE PER SERVING

Calories: 160

Fat: 5g

Protein: 4g

Carbohydrates: 28g

Breakfast Green Smoothie

SERVING SIZE

One person

COOKING TIME

5 minutes

INGREDIENTS

Banana: 1

Baby spinach: 1 cup

Fat free milk: ½ cup

Whole oats: ¼ cup

Mango: ¾ cup

Nonfat yogurt: ¼ cup

Vanilla: ½ tsp

PREPARATION

1. Blend all ingredients until smooth
2. Serve chilled.

NUTRITIONAL VALUE PER SERVING

Calories: 350

Fat: 2g

Protein: 12g

Carbohydrates: 77g

Almond Date Shake

SERVING SIZE

4 persons

COOKING TIME

10 minutes

INGREDIENTS

Chopped dates: 1/3 cup

Warm water: 2 tbsp

Vanilla almond milk: 2 cups

Fat-free dairy yogurt: ½ cup

Ripe banana: 1

Ice cubes: as desired

Ground nutmeg: 1/8 tsp

PREPARATION

1. Soak dates in warm water for 5 minutes to soften
2. Combine all ingredients in blender and blend until smooth and frothy.
3. Pour into tall glasses and serve.

NUTRITIONAL VALUE PER SERVING

Calories: 142

Fat: 2g

Protein: 3g

Carbohydrates: 28g

Berry Museli

SERVING SIZE

4 persons

COOKING TIME

Preparation time: 5 minutes

Refrigeration: 6 hours

*prepare overnight and refrigerate to have at breakfast instantly.

INGREDIENTS

Rolled oats: 1 cup

Fruit yogurt: 1 cup

Milk: ½ cup

Dried fruit: ½ cup (raisins, apricots, dates)

Chopped apple: ½ cup

Frozen blueberries: ½ cup

Toasted walnuts: ¼ cup

Salt: a pinch

PREPARATION

1. Mix oats, yogurt, salt, and milk and refrigerate for 6 hours.
2. Mix in dried and fresh fruit.
3. Served sprinkled with chopped nuts.

NUTRITIONAL VALUE PER SERVING

Calories: 170

Fat: 5g

Protein: 6g

Carbohydrates: 27g

Quinoa

SERVING SIZE

4 persons

COOKING TIME

15 minutes

INGREDIENTS

Low fat milk: 2 cups

Quinoa: 1 cup

Honey: ¼ cup

Cinnamon: ¼ tsp

Sliced almonds: ¼ cup

Chopped dried apricots: ¼ cup

PREPARATION

1. Boil quinoa in milk after rinsing through water thoroughly.
2. Simmer until most liquid is absorbed.
3. Fluff with fork after removing from heat and stir in remaining ingredients
4. Serve fresh

NUTRITIONAL VALUE PER SERVING

Calories: 320

Fat: 5g

Protein: 12g

Carbohydrates: 59g

Broccoli and Cheese Omelet

SERVING SIZE

9 persons

COOKING TIME

15 minutes

INGREDIENTS

Broccoli florets: 4 cups

Eggs: 4

Egg whites: 1 cup

Reduced fat cheddar: ¼ cup

Parmesan cheese: ¼ cup

Olive oil: 1 tbsp

Cooking spray

Salt and pepper

PREPARATION

1. Steam broccoli and mash adding oil, salt, and pepper. Mix well.
2. Spoon broccoli mixture onto baking tray, sprayed with cooking spray.
3. Add and mix egg whites and parmesan cheese in a small bowl and add to the mixture
4. Bake in preheated oven to 350 degrees for about 15 minutes
5. Serve fresh

NUTRITIONAL VALUE PER SERVING

Calories: 104

Fat: 7g

Protein: 9g

Carbohydrates: 3g

Morning Mohito

SERVING SIZE

6 persons

COOKING TIME

10 minutes

INGREDIENTS

Dark honey: ½ cup

Lime juice: ½ cup

Mint leaves: ½ cup

Grapefruit juice: 2 cups

Orange juice: 2 cups

Grated lime zest: 2 tsp

Lime: 1 (cut into pieces)

PREPARATION

1. Combine honey and lime juice in small saucepan and bring to boil. Add mint leaves and remove from heat, steep mixture for 5 minutes.
2. Combine all ingredients in large pitcher and stir well.
3. Serve in tall glasses with ice.

NUTRITIONAL VALUE PER SERVING

Calories: 168

Fat: 0g

Protein: 1g

Carbohydrates: 41g

Cinnamon French toast

SERVING SIZE

2 persons

COOKING TIME

10 minutes

INGREDIENTS

Egg whites: 4

Vanilla: 1 tsp

Ground nutmeg: 1/8 tsp

Cinnamon bread: 4 slices

Powdered sugar: 2 tsp

Maple syrup: ¼ cup

PREPARATION

1. Combine and whisk egg whites, vanilla and nutmeg in a small bowl,
2. Dip bread into mixture and coat both sides.
3. Over medium heat, place a nonstick frying pan and add bread when a drop of water sizzles at it hits the pan.
4. Sprinkle with cinnamon and cook both sides until golden brown about 4 minutes each side.
5. Serve toasts with maple syrup.

NUTRITIONAL VALUE PER SERVING

Calories: 295

Fat: 2g

Protein: 12g

Carbohydrates: 56g

Apple-Swiss Panini

SERVING SIZE

Four persons

COOKING TIME

10 minutes

INGREDIENTS

Whole grain bread: 8 slices

Non-fat honey mustard: ¼ cup

Thinly sliced crisp apples: 2

Low-fat Swiss cheese: thinly sliced 6 ounces

Arugula leaves: 1 cup

Cooking spray

PREPARATION

1. Spread honey mustard, topped with a layer of apple slices, cheese and arugula leaves over four slices of bread.
2. Top each bread slice with the remaining bread slices and grill for 3 minutes on each side until bread is toasted.
3. Serve after it is slight cooled.

NUTRITIONAL VALUE PER SERVING

Calories: 280

Fat: 4.5g

Protein: 17g

Carbohydrates: 44g

Orange Rice Salad

SERVING SIZE

7 persons

COOKING TIME

10 minutes

INGREDIENTS

Cooked brown rice: 2 cups

Diced celery: ½ cup

Raisins: ¾ cup

Chopped nuts: ¼ cup

Canola oil: 2 tbsp

Orange juice: 1 tbsp

Parsley: ¼ cup

Green onions: 3 (chopped)

Mandarin oranges: 1 can

Pepper to taste

PREPARATION

1. Mix all ingredients in bowl, toss well.
2. Serve immediately.

NUTRITIONAL VALUE PER SERVING

Calories: 200

Fat: 7g

Protein: 3g

Carbohydrates: 32g

Sunshine Wraps

SERVING SIZE

Four persons

COOKING TIME

15 minutes

INGREDIENTS

One large chicken breast: 8 oz

Diced celery: ½ cup

Canned mandarin oranges: 2/3 cup

Minced onion: ¼ cup

Mayonnaise: 2 tbsp

Soy sauce: 1 tsp

Garlic powder: ¼ tsp

Black pepper: ¼ tsp

Whole-wheat tortilla: 1 large

Lettuce leaves: 4 large

PREPARATION

1. Cook chicken breast over medium-high heat in a large pan until done throughout and cut into cubes after it has cooled.
2. Mix chicken, celery, oranges, and onions in a medium bowl. Add mayonnaise, soy sauce, garlic, and pepper and mix gently.
3. Cut the tortilla into four quarters and lay down one lettuce leaf on each.
4. Put ¼ of chicken mixture on each leaf, roll the tortillas into a cone and it is ready to serve.

NUTRITIONAL VALUE PER SERVING

Calories: 192

Fat: 5g

Protein: 16g

Carbohydrates: 20g

Salmon Salad Pita

SERVING SIZE

Three persons

COOKING TIME

10 minutes

INGREDIENTS

Canned Alaskan salmon: ¾ cup

Fat-free yogurt: 3 tbsp

Lemon juice: 1 tbsp

Minced red bell pepper: 2 tbsp

Minced red onion: 1 tbsp

Chopped capers: 1 tsp

Fresh or dried dill: a pinch

Black pepper: to taste

Lettuce leaves: 3

Whole-wheat pita bread: 3 pieces

PREPARATION

1. To make salmon salad, mix all ingredients together except lettuce leaves and pita bread.
2. Place lettuce leaf and 1/3 cup salad inside each pita and serve.

NUTRITIONAL VALUE PER SERVING

Calories: 180

Fat: 4g

Protein: 19g

Carbohydrates: 19g

Mayo-Less Tuna Salad

SERVING SIZE

Two persons

COOKING TIME

10 minutes

INGREDIENTS

Tuna: 5 oz can

Extra virgin olive oil: 1 tbsp

Red wine vinegar: 1 tbsp

Chopped green onion tops: ¼ cup

Arugula: 2 cups

Cooked pasta: 1 cup

Parmesan cheese: 1 tbsp

Black pepper: to taste

PREPARATION

1. Toss tuna with oil, vinegar, onion, arugula and cooked pasta in a large bowl.
2. Divide in two plates and serve immediately with pepper and parmesan cheese

NUTRITIONAL VALUE PER SERVING

Calories: 245

Fat: 7g

Protein: 23g

Carbohydrates: 23g

Pear, Turkey and Cheese Sandwich

SERVING SIZE

Two persons

COOKING TIME

10 minutes

INGREDIENTS

Multi grain sandwich bread: 2 slices

Dijon style mustard: 2 tsp

Reduced sodium cooked turkey: 2 slices

Thinly sliced pear: 1

Low fat shredded mozzarella cheese: ¼ cup

Pepper: to taste

PREPARATION

1. Spread bread slices with mustard, cover with turkey and pear slices. Sprinkle cheese and pepper
2. Grill the sandwich for 2 minutes on each side and serve warm.

NUTRITIONAL VALUE PER SERVING

Calories: 190

Fat: 4g

Protein: 13g

Carbohydrates: 28g

Orange Rice Salad

SERVING SIZE

Seven persons

COOKING TIME

15 minutes

INGREDIENTS

Cooked brown rice: 2 cups

Celery: ½ cup

Raisins: ¾ cup

Chopped nuts: ¼ cup

Canola oil: 2 tbsp

Orange juice: 1 tbsp

Chopped parsley: ¼ cup

Thinly sliced green onions: 3

Mandarin oranges with juice: 1 can

Pepper: to taste

PREPARATION

1. Mix all ingredients in a bowl
2. Allow to cool for 15 minutes and serve cold.

NUTRITIONAL VALUE PER SERVING

Calories: 200

Fat: 7g

Protein: 3g

Carbohydrates: 32g

Veggie Quesadillas with Cilantro Yogurt Dip

SERVING SIZE

Four persons

COOKING TIME

10-15 minutes

INGREDIENTS

Black beans: 1 cup

Chopped cilantro: 2 tbsp

Chopped bell pepper: ½

Corn kernels: ½ cup

Low fat shredded cheese: 1 cup

Soft corn tortillas: 6

Shredded carrot: 1

Minced jalapeno pepper: ½

Cilantro yogurt dip:

Non-fat yogurt: 1 cup

Chopped cilantro: 2 tbsp

Lime juice: 1 tbsp

PREPARATION

1. Place cheese, corn, beans, cilantro, shredded carrots, and peppers on each tortilla.
2. Warm tortillas over low heat, until golden for 2 minutes on each side.
3. In separate bowl, mix ingredients for the dip.
4. Cut the quesadilla into equal pieces and serve.

NUTRITIONAL VALUE PER SERVING

Calories: 240

Fat: 2g

Protein: 17g

Carbohydrates: 42g

Yellow Lentils

SERVING SIZE

4 persons

COOKING TIME

15 minutes

INGREDIENTS

Black sesame seeds: 1 tsp

Olive oil: 1 tbsp

Minced shallot: 1

Ground ginger: 1 tsp

Curry powder: ½ tsp

Ground turmeric: ½ tsp

Yellow lentils: 1 cup

Vegetable stock: 1 ½ cup

Light coconut milk: 1/2 cup

Baby spinach leaves: 2 cups

Salt: ½ tsp

Fresh cilantro: 1 tbsp

PREPARATION

1. Toast sesame seeds over medium heat and remove when brown.
2. Heat olive oil, and add shallot, ginger, curry powder and turmeric, stir for about 1 minute.
3. Add lentils and coconut milk and bring to boil on high heat. Simmer for 12 minutes on low heat until lentils become tender.
4. Stir in spinach for about 3 minutes and serve hot.

NUTRITIONAL VALUE PER SERVING

Calories: 243

Fat: 7g

Protein: 13g

Carbohydrates: 32g

Grilled Cod with Salad

SERVING SIZE

2 persons

COOKING TIME

15 minutes

INGREDIENTS

Broiled cod: 6 ounces

Olive oil: 1 ½ tbsp

Shredded spinach: 1 ½ cup

Shredded kohlrabi: 1 ½ cup

Shredded celery: 1 cup

Shredded carrot: 1 ½ cup

Fresh basil: 2bsp

Fresh parsley: 1 tbsp

Chopped red bell pepper: ¾ cup

Lemon juice and zest of 1 lemon

Lime juice and zest of 1 lime

Orange juice and zest of 1 orange

Grapefruit segments: 1 cup

Orange segments: ½ cup

PREPARATION

1. Spray grill with cooking spray and place cod brushed lightly with oil
2. Grill cod for about 4 minutes.
3. Toss remaining ingredients in a bowl and mix well, except grapefruit and orange segments.
4. Serve cod with salad and citrus pieces divided into two plates, topped with citrus pieces.

NUTRITIONAL VALUE PER SERVING

Calories: 412

Fat: 12g

Protein: 26g

Carbohydrates: 50g

White Chicken Chili

SERVING SIZE

8 persons

COOKING TIME

15 minutes

INGREDIENTS

White chunk chicken: 1 can

Cooked white beans: 3 cups

Low sodium diced tomatoes: 1 can

Low sodium chicken broth: 4 cups

Chopped onion: 1 medium

Chopped green pepper: ½ medium

Chopped red pepper: 1 medium

Minced garlic cloves: 2

Chili powder: 2 tsp

Ground cumin: 1 tsp

Oregano: 1 tsp

Reduced fat shredded cheese: 6 tbsp

Cilantro: 3 tbsp

Low fat baked tortilla chips: 6 ounces

Cayenne pepper: to taste

PREPARATION

1. Add chicken, beans, tomatoes and chicken broth. Simmer over medium heat.
2. Add onions, peppers, and garlic in a nonstick frying pan. Sauté until soft for about 3 minutes.
3. Add onion and pepper mixture to broth, stir in chili powder, cumin, oregano and simmer for 10 minutes.
4. Add in bowls and serve with cheese and cilantro sprinkled on top.

NUTRITIONAL VALUE PER SERVING

Calories: 268

Fat: 1g

Protein: 19g

Carbohydrates: 41g

Chinese Noodles with Vegetables

SERVING SIZE

4 persons

COOKING TIME

15 minutes

INGREDIENTS

Chinese noodles: 1 package

Peanut oil: 1 tbsp

Sesame oil: 1 tbsp

Fresh ginger: 1 tbsp

Chopped garlic cloves: 2

Reduced sodium soy sauce: 2 tbsp

Broccoli florets: 1 cup

Bean sprouts: 1 cup

Cherry tomatoes (halved): 8

Chopped spinach: 1 cup

Chopped scallions: 2

Red chili flakes: crushed

PREPARATION

1. Prepare noodles according to package instructions, drain thoroughly, and set aside.
2. Over medium heat cook and stir ginger, garlic, soy sauce, and broccoli. Add remaining vegetables and noodles in oil. Toss well until warmed through.
3. Top with red chili flakes and serve immediately.

NUTRITIONAL VALUE PER SERVING

Calories: 270

Fat: 9g

Protein: 9g

Carbohydrates: 38g

Acorn Squash with Apples

SERVING SIZE

2 persons

COOKING TIME

10 minutes

INGREDIENTS

Granny smith apple: 1 (sliced)

Brown sugar: 2 tbsp

Acorn squash: 1 small

Trans free margarine: 2 tsp

PREPARATION

1. Mix apple and brown sugar in bowl and set aside
2. Pierce squash with knife for steam to escape during cooking. Microwave for 5 minutes and turn after 3 minutes to evenly cook on all sides.
3. Cut squash into half and discard seeds, fill the hollowed squash with apple mixture and cook it in microwave for about 2 minutes more.
4. Top with margarine and serve immediately.

NUTRITIONAL VALUE PER SERVING

Calories: 270

Fat: 6g

Protein: 2g

Carbohydrates: 52g

Easy Cheesy Enchiladas

SERVING SIZE

Sixteen persons

COOKING TIME

15 minutes

INGREDIENTS

Black beans: Two cans

Salsa: ½ cup

Reduced fat shredded cheese: 1 ½ cup

Whole-wheat flour tortillas: eight

Enchilada sauce: One can

PREPARATION

1. Preheat oven to 350 degrees
2. In a bowl, mix beans, salsa, and half cheese. In each tortilla, spoon ½ cup of bean mixture. Roll and place in baking dish.
3. Pour enchilada sauce and sprinkle remaining cheese over tortillas and bake for 15 minutes.

NUTRITIONAL VALUE PER SERVING

Calories: 170

Fat: 5g

Protein: 8g

Carbohydrates: 23g

Festive Cranberry Chicken

SERVING SIZE

Four persons

COOKING TIME

15 minutes

INGREDIENTS

Boneless chicken breasts: 1 pound

Butter: 1 tsp

Black pepper: ¼ tsp

Cranberry sauce: ¾ cup

Chili sauce: ¼ cup

Apple juice: ¼ cup

Brown sugar: 1 tsp

PREPARATION

1. Slightly pounced chicken and sprinkle with pepper
2. Brown the chicken in butter, in a large pan. Add remaining ingredients and simmer for 15 minutes.
3. Remove lid and boil sauce to desired thickness. Serve warm.

NUTRITIONAL VALUE PER SERVING

Calories: 302

Fat: 5g

Protein: 35g

Carbohydrates: 27g

Garden Quesadillas

SERVING SIZE

Five persons

COOKING TIME

15 minutes

INGREDIENTS

Sweet peppers: 2 small

Thinly cut red onion: 1 small

Olive oil: 2 tsp

Ground cumin: ½ tsp

Chili powder: ½ tsp

Cilantro: 2 tbsp

Fat free cream cheese: 1/3 cup

Flour tortillas: 5

Salsa: ¼ cup

PREPARATION

1. Cook sweet peppers and onion in 1 tsp oil for 3 minutes. Stir in cumin, chili powder, and cilantro and stir for 2 minutes.
2. Spread cream cheese over each tortilla and add pepper mixture.
3. Fold tortillas in half and bake for 5 minutes in oven at 425 degree F.
4. Serve the quesadilla, cut into 4 wedges with salsa.

NUTRITIONAL VALUE PER SERVING

Calories: 58

Fat: 2g

Protein: 2g

Carbohydrates: 8g

Cilantro Lime Tilapia Tacos

SERVING SIZE

Four persons

COOKING TIME

15 minutes

INGREDIENTS

Tilapia filets: 1 pound

Olive oil: 1 tsp

Chopped onion: 1 small

Minced garlic cloves: 4

Chopped jalapeno peppers: 2

Diced tomatoes: 2 cups

Chopped cilantro: ¼ cup

Lime juice: 3 tbsp

Salt and pepper: to taste

White corn tortillas: 8

Sliced avocado: 1 medium

Shredded cabbage: 1cup

Lime wedges: for garnish

PREPARATION

1. Mix onion and garlic to olive oil on heated oven.
2. Cook tilapia until flesh starts to flake and add limejuice, cilantro, tomatoes, jalapeno peppers.
3. Cook for 5 minutes over medium high heat and add salt and pepper
4. Heat tortillas in the meantime on each side to warm.
5. Serve ¼ cup of fish with two slices of avocado on each tortilla.
6. Top with shredded cabbage and lime wedges and serve.

NUTRITIONAL VALUE PER SERVING

Calories: 427

Fat: 12g

Protein: 35g

Carbohydrates: 45g

One Pan Spaghetti

SERVING SIZE

Ten persons

COOKING TIME

15 minutes

INGREDIENTS

Lean ground beef: ½ pound

Chopped onion: 1 medium

Water: 3 ½ cups

Tomato sauce: 1 can

Dried oregano: 2 tsp

Sugar, garlic powder, and rosemary: ½ tsp each

Pepper: ¼ tsp

Broken spaghetti: 2 cups

Shredded cheese: 1 cup

PREPARATION

1. Over medium high heat, brown beef and onions.
2. Stir in water, tomato sauce, and spices
3. When it comes to boil add spaghetti, and cover pan for 10-15 minutes.
4. Top with grated cheese when spaghetti is tender and serve

NUTRITIONAL VALUE PER SERVING

Calories: 230

Fat: 6g

Protein: 13g

Carbohydrates: 31g

Cheeseburgers

SERVING SIZE

Four persons

COOKING TIME

15 minutes

INGREDIENTS

Ground beef: 1 pound

Quick cooking oats: 2 tbsp

Steak seasoning blend: ½ tsp

Wheat hamburger buns: 4

Low fat cheese: 4 slices

PREPARATION

1. Crush oats to a fine consistency
2. Mix ground beef, oats, steak seasoning blend in bowl thoroughly, and shape into patties.
3. Grill the patties for 12 minutes over medium heat
4. Serve with cheese slices lined in burgers.

NUTRITIONAL VALUE PER SERVING

Calories: 318

Fat: 10g

Protein: 33g

Carbohydrates: 24g

Cowboy Salad

SERVING SIZE

12 persons

COOKING TIME

15 minutes

INGREDIENTS

Black beans: 2 cans (15 ounce each)

Corn: 1 can

Cilantro: to taste

Green onions: 5

Medium tomatoes: 3

Avocado: 1

Olive oil: 1 tbsp

Lime juice: 2 tbsp

Salt and pepper: to taste

PREPARATION

1. Rinse the corn and black beans. Chop cilantro and green onion, dice avocados and tomatoes. Combine all ingredients in bowl.
2. Mix oil, lime juice, salt and pepper and pour over salad. Toss well.

NUTRITIONAL VALUE PER SERVING

Calories: 70

Fat: 2.5g

Protein: 2g

Carbohydrates: 9g

Pasta and Broccoli

SERVING SIZE

6 persons

COOKING TIME

15 minutes

INGREDIENTS

Pasta: 12 ounces

Broccoli florets: 6 ½ cups

Chopped garlic cloves: 5

Parmesan cheese: ¼ cup

Olive oil: 2 tbsp

Salt and pepper: to taste

PREPARATION

1. Add pasta and broccoli to boiled water and cook. Drain and set aside when done.
2. Add garlic to 1 tbsp of oil over high heat, cook until golden. Reduce heat and add pasta back, mix well.
3. Add remaining olive oil, salt and pepper and serve.

NUTRITIONAL VALUE PER SERVING

Calories: 289

Fat: 7g

Protein: 12g

Carbohydrates: 48g

Citrus Chicken

SERVING SIZE

10 persons

COOKING TIME

15 minutes

INGREDIENTS

Olive oil: 2 tsp

Cubed chicken breast: 3

Ground ginger: ½ tsp

Minced garlic clove: 1

Pineapple chunks with juice: 1 can

Orange juice: 1 ½ cup

Reduced sodium chicken broth: 1 cup

Vinegar: 2 tbsp

Sliced vegetables: 4 cups (celery, green peppers, onions and mushrooms)

Tomato wedges: 1 medium

Reduced sodium soy sauce: 2 tbsp

Sugar: 1 tbsp

Cornstarch: 2 tbsp

PREPARATION

1. Heat oil and add chicken, ginger, and garlic for 5 minutes.
2. Add pineapple juice, orange juice, chicken broth and vinegar and simmer for 5 minutes.
3. Add vegetables and mix remaining ingredients, stir well and let mixture thicken.
4. Serve immediately.

NUTRITIONAL VALUE PER SERVING

Calories: 110

Fat: 2g

Protein: 9g

Carbohydrates: 13g

Pear Chicken Curry

SERVING SIZE

6 persons

COOKING TIME

15 minutes

INGREDIENTS

Ripe pears, divided: 2

Olive oil: 1 tbsp

Dice onion: 1 cup

Curry powder: 1 tbsp

Minced garlic: 1 tsp

Salt: 1 tsp

Ground ginger: ¾ tsp

Ground cinnamon: ¾ tsp

Ground black pepper: ¼ tsp

Cubed chicken breast: 3

Light coconut milk: 1 can

Raisins: 1/3 cup

PREPARATION

1. Peel and core 1 pear and set aside. Add onion, curry powder, garlic, salt, ginger, cinnamon, and pepper in oil and sauté 5 minutes. Stir occasionally.
2. Add chicken, pureed pear, coconut milk, and raisins, and simmer for 5 minutes. Cut remaining pear into cubes and add to curry.
3. Serve immediately.

NUTRITIONAL VALUE PER SERVING

Calories: 272

Fat: 10g

Protein: 24g

Carbohydrates: 20g

Vegetable and Turkey Stir-Fry

SERVING SIZE

8 persons

COOKING TIME

15 minutes

INGREDIENTS

Olive oil: 1 tbsp

Salt: ½ tsp

Minced ginger root: thin slices

Garlic powder: 1/8 tsp

Turkey cubes: 1 cup

Chopped vegetables: 2 cups (celery, mushroom, water chestnuts, bok choy)

Cooked brown rice: 3 cups

PREPARATION

1. Stir-fry salt, ginger root, garlic, turkey and vegetables in oil over medium heat, until vegetables become tender.
2. Serve over cooked rice.

NUTRITIONAL VALUE PER SERVING

Calories: 150

Fat: 4g

Protein: 10g

Carbohydrates: 20g

Chicken Cabbage Stir Fry

SERVING SIZE

6 persons

COOKING TIME

15 minutes

INGREDIENTS

Chicken breast: 3

Olive oil: 1 tsp

Shredded green cabbage: 3 cups

Cornstarch: 1 tbsp

Ground ginger: ½ tsp

Garlic powder: ¼ tsp

Water: ½ cup

Low sodium soy sauce: 1 tbsp

PREPARATION

1. Cut chicken breast into strips and stir-fry over medium heat in oil. Tun constantly until done.
2. Add cabbage and sauté for 2 minutes
3. Mix cornstarch, water and soy sauce until smooth and stir into mixture
4. Cook for 1 minute until chicken is coated and sauce is thick
5. Serve immediately.

NUTRITIONAL VALUE PER SERVING

Calories: 90

Fat: 2.5g

Protein: 13g

Carbohydrates: 4g

Bean Dip Athenos

SERVING SIZE

Twenty-four persons

COOKING TIME

10 minutes

INGREDIENTS

Cooked garbanzo beans: 2 15 ounce cans

Fat free sour cream: 2/3 cup

Minced garlic: 2 tsp

Balsamic vinegar: 4 tbsp

Chopped tomatoes: ¼ cup

Chopped parsley: ¼ cup

Chopped olives: 2 tbsp

Assorted vegetables and crackers: for serving

PREPARATION

1. Blend beans, sour cream, garlic, and vinegar until smooth. Add tomatoes, parsley, and chopped olives, stir well.
2. Serve the dip with assorted vegetables and crackers.

NUTRITIONAL VALUE PER SERVING

Calories: 54

Fat: 1g

Protein: 2g

Carbohydrates: 10g

Pumpkin Pie Spiced Yogurt

SERVING SIZE

Two persons

COOKING TIME

10 minutes

INGREDIENTS

Low fat yogurt: 2 cups

Pumpkin puree: ½ cup

Cinnamon: ¼ tsp

Pumpkin pie spice: ¼ tsp

Chopped walnuts: ¼ cup

Honey: to drizzle

PREPARATION

1. Mix the pumpkin puree with spices thoroughly and add yogurt.
2. Sprinkle with walnuts and honey to serve.

NUTRITIONAL VALUE PER SERVING

Calories: 237

Fat: 10g

Protein: 15g

Carbohydrates: 24g

Lemon Smoothie

SERVING SIZE

One person

COOKING TIME

5 minutes

INGREDIENTS

Fat free yogurt: 1 container

Granulated sugar: 2 tbsp

Lemon juice: 1 tsp

Grated lemon zest: ½ tsp

PREPARATION

1. Blend all ingredients together until smooth
2. Serve chilled

NUTRITIONAL VALUE PER SERVING

Calories: 190

Fat: 1g

Protein: 13g

Carbohydrates: 36g

Muffins

SERVING SIZE

Twelve persons

COOKING TIME

15 minutes

INGREDIENTS

Cooking spray

Egg: 1

Low fat milk: 1 cup

Sugar: 1/3 cup

Olive oil: 2 tbsp

Grated carrots: ½ cup

Raisins: ½ cup

Toasted walnuts: ½ cup (optional)

Vanilla: 1 tsp

Flour: 1 ½ cup

Oatmeal: 1 cup

Cinnamon: 1 tsp

Baking powder: 1 tsp

Baking soda: ½ tsp

Salt: ½ tsp

PREPARATION

1. Preheat oven to 400 degrees.
2. Mix egg, milk, oil, sugar, carrots, raisins, walnuts, and vanilla in a bowl.
3. Separately, mix flour, oatmeal, cinnamon, baking powder, baking soda, and salt.
4. Add wet to dry ingredients and stir gently.
5. Fill muffin cups with batter and bake for 15 minutes.

NUTRITIONAL VALUE PER SERVING

Calories: 180

Fat: 6g

Protein: 4g

Carbohydrates: 26g

Zucchini Pizza Bites

SERVING SIZE

One person

COOKING TIME

10-15 minutes

INGREDIENTS

Large zucchini: 4 slices

Olive oil

Pepper

Pizza sauce: 4 tbsp

Shredded mozzarella cheese: 2 tbsp

PREPARATION

1. Pre heat broiler to 500 degree F
2. Brush both sides of zucchini slices with olive oil and drizzle pepper.
3. Place slices in broiler for 2 minutes for each side
4. Remove slices and spread each slice with pizza sauce and cheese
5. Broil again until cheese melts. Serve warm.

NUTRITIONAL VALUE PER SERVING

Calories: 69

Fat: 4g

Protein: 5g

Carbohydrates: 5g

Melon Cooler

SERVING SIZE

3 persons

COOKING TIME

5 minutes

INGREDIENTS

Cubed cantaloupe: 2 cups

Low fat lemon yogurt: 1 cup

Orange juice: 1 cup

PREPARATION

1. Mix all ingredients in blender and blend until smooth
2. Serve chilled

NUTRITIONAL VALUE PER SERVING

Calories: 120

Fat: 1g

Protein: 5g

Carbohydrates: 22g

Skillet Granola

SERVING SIZE

24 persons

COOKING TIME

10-15 minutes

INGREDIENTS

Olive oil: 1/3 cup

Honey: 3 tbsp

Powdered milk: ¼ cup

Vanilla: 1 tsp

Oats: 4 cups

Sunflower seeds: ½ cup

Raisins: 1 cup

PREPARATION

1. Over medium heat warm oil and honey and add powdered milk. Stir in oats and sunflower seeds and mix well. Stir until oatmeal is brown.
2. Stir in raisins after taking off heat and pour mixture on baking sheet. Let it cool and store in airtight container.

NUTRITIONAL VALUE PER SERVING

Calories: 120

Fat: 5g

Protein: 3g

Carbohydrates: 17g

Chicken Burritos

SERVING SIZE

4 persons

COOKING TIME

10-15 minutes

INGREDIENTS

Olive oil: 1 tsp

Chopped red bell pepper: 1

Chopped jalapeno pepper: 1

Chopped celery: 2 ribs

Chopped onion: 1

Cumin seeds: 2 tbsp

Grape tomatoes: 1 pint

Oregano: 2 tbsp

Chopped garlic: 2 cloves

Chicken breast meat: 8 ounces

Whole wheat tortillas: 4

Cheddar cheese: ½ cup

Shredded green cabbage: 2 cups

PREPARATION

1. Sauté peppers, celery, onion, and cumin in oil over medium heat for 5 minutes. Add tomatoes, oregano and garlic, continue to sauté.
2. Blend ingredients until desired consistency
3. Divide breast meat from chicken among tortillas.
4. Top with cheese and cabbage and enjoy.

NUTRITIONAL VALUE PER SERVING

Calories: 333

Fat: 13g

Protein: 26g

Carbohydrates: 28g

Tuna Pita Pockets

SERVING SIZE

6 persons

COOKING TIME

10-13 minutes

INGREDIENTS

Romaine lettuce: 1 ½ cup

Diced tomatoes: ¾ cup

Chopped green bell peppers: ½ cup

Shredded carrots: ½ cup

Finely chopped broccoli: ½ cup

Chopped onion: ¼ cup

Low salt white tuna: 2 cans

Low fat ranch dressing: ½ cup

Whole wheat pita pockets: 3 whole (cut in half)

PREPARATION

1. Add and mix lettuce, tomatoes, peppers, carrots, broccoli and onions
2. Add tuna and ranch dressing in separate bowl and mix well. Combine both mixtures.
3. Place ¾ cup of tuna salad into each pita pocket and serve.

NUTRITIONAL VALUE PER SERVING

Calories: 199

Fat: 5g

Protein: 15g

Carbohydrates: 23g

Garlic Potatoes

SERVING SIZE

8 persons

COOKING TIME

15 minutes

INGREDIENTS

Boiled potato cubes: 3 pounds

Garlic cloves: 6

Fat free milk: 1 tbsp

Trans fat free margarine: 1 tbsp

Black pepper: to taste

Parsley: 2 tbsp (chopped)

PREPARATION

1. Boil garlic and water and drain the garlic when tender.
2. Combine garlic and milk in blender, puree until smooth.
3. Add margarine and garlic puree to potatoes and mash to desired consistency
4. Season with black pepper and serve with parsley

NUTRITIONAL VALUE PER SERVING

Calories: 157

Fat: 5g

Protein: 2g

Carbohydrates: 24g

Apple and Pistachio Salad

SERVING SIZE

4 persons

COOKING TIME

10-12 minutes

INGREDIENTS

Low fat yogurt: 1 cup

Cubed granny smith apples: 3

Pistachios: 1/3 cup

Blue cheese crumbles: 1/3 cup

Lemon juice

Cayenne pepper: ¼ tsp

Black pepper: ½ tsp

PREPARATION

1. Mix yogurt and pepper, squeeze lemon juice onto apple, and add to yogurt.
2. Garnish with blue cheese and pistachios, mix well and serve.

NUTRITIONAL VALUE PER SERVING

Calories: 200

Fat: 8.5g

Protein: 8.5g

Carbohydrates: 25g

Pumpkin Chai Smoothie

SERVING SIZE

Four persons

COOKING TIME

10 minutes

INGREDIENTS

Milk: 1 cup

Unsweetened instant tea: 1 tbsp

Pumpkin pie spice: ½ tsp

Ground cardamom: ¼ tsp

Banana: 1

Fat free vanilla yogurt: 3/4 cup

Canned pumpkin: ½ cup

Maple syrup: 1 tbsp

Ice cubes: 1 cup

PREPARATION

1. Combine milk, instant tea, spices, and blends until is dissolved.
2. Add remaining ingredients and blend until smooth.
3. Pour into glasses and serve chilled.

NUTRITIONAL VALUE PER SERVING

Calories: 118

Fat: 0g

Protein: 5.6g

Carbohydrates: 24g

Made in the USA
Middletown, DE
30 June 2015